MW01172381

Praise for *New Sp*

"I loved reading Tamsin's Spenser Smith's *New Species of Color*. I was immediately drawn into the irresistibly mysterious and original worlds of these poems: their charms, their sly humor, their precise questions and generous, open, suggestions of answers. Deeply intelligent, these are the poems of a contemporary heir to Wallace Stevens, were he kinder and more open to love."

— Matthew Zapruder, *Story of a Poem* and *I Love Hearing Your Dreams*

"The penultimate poem in Tamsin Smith's marvelous new collection, begins, "She draws lines like horizons"—a statement that aptly applies to Smith herself, in that her lines of poetry brilliantly limn the seen and the unseen. Smith is a keen observer of light of love of sky of skin of color of consciousness. The poems of *New Species of Color* masterfully move from what she regards to what she beholds. Everything is alive and glowing and moving and becoming. As a reader, I know I am in the hands of someone who is feeling her way through the world the way she is feeling her way through language, which is to say with alacrity and awe. I love this book."

— Dean Rader, *Before the Borderless: Dialogues with the Art of Cy Twombly* and *Self-Portrait as Wikipedia Entry*

"'Nothing fails to indicate' writes Tamsin Smith in her beguiling *New Species of Color*. In poems full of mystery and of mysterious vectors Smith (who is also a visual artist) creates canvases that have 'never a dull tongue blade' and which invite us 'to stop dividing the universe.' This is a shimmering, inventive book."

— Tess Taylor, *Leaning Towards the Light* and *Rift Zone*

NEW SPECIES OF COLOR

New Species of Color

Tamsin Spencer Smith

San Francisco, California

ISBN: 979-8-9894133-3-1

Versions of "Winter Poem", "Fall Poem", "Spring Poem", and "Summer Poem" first appeared as part of the *Entanglement* catalogue for artist Hollis Heichemer (New York: Hollis Taggart Gallery, 2021).

The final line of "Red Verónica" is taken from *All that's Left* by Jack Hirschman (San Francisco: City Lights, 2008).

"Prophecy" was first published in Volume Poetry, (Vol 2, Issue 4, 2022).

"Not to Squander the Gazing" was first published in Reverberations II (Sebastopol: RiskPress Foundation, 2022).

"Two in a Balance of Long Exposure" was first published in *Reverberations III* as a response to Edward Weston's photograph "Shells" (Sebastopol: RiskPress Foundation, 2023).

A selection of earlier versions of these poems were included in a chapbook titled *Sista Shine* hand-stitched and hand-painted by the author in an edition of 50 (2023).

Cover Art by William Theophilus Brown

Author Photo by Christopher Michel

San Francisco, California

I grew in green
slide and slant
of shore and shade

~ Loraine Niedeker

First the air is blue and then
it is bluer and then green and then
black I am blacking out and yet
my mask is powerful

~ Adrienne Rich

I found I could say things with colors that
I couldn't say in any other way –
things that I had no words for.

~ Georgia O'Keeffe

Here is my box of new crayons at your feet

~ Marge Piercy

CONTENTS

MOIRA

Good lives are governed by probability
Every pencil makes its mark

Salt falls from the nets of fishermen
Our eyes draw the remains of a wide sea

Hands will move like dark winged scavengers
Sky talk becomes a circling omen

Shade on the starched page grows longer
Impatient as a spring bud, an adoring lover

Pretend that you know nothing of war
The first eyes of the world blink

Fey to the soldier of time
You walk across deep roots at the shore

See the yellow moon crack upon the sand
Fried full with grit and ground stronger

Never dull the tongue-blade
Search beneath the shells

Those tangled weeds invite the body
To stop dividing the universe

THINGS I KNOW

The residue of absence creates a sense of place.

Relocation stimulates growth.

Replacement of commas with the short oblique stroke of the virgule thickens the plot.

Do not ignore a loaded brush,

A turning leaf.

Light shattered in the snow may be the essence of beauty, but gravity resides in imitative counterpoint.

Self-portraiture is simply a metrical position equated with anonymity.

Nothing fails to indicate (pause to take that in)

Stasis is to should as quicksand is to could.

A half-way halo still shines plus

I have lived a thousand nights face to face with the sinking sun.

I have run far from the hues that best become me

& back again & again & again to amber

WINTER POEM

as rites of purification
the old year melts by

quicker than dynamite
splits lovely brittle sticks

or hard miles holler in
hunger at lost chances

breathless diction excuses
a silent eloquence to slip

beneath ice and uncertainty
in search of new moons

I am, have had enough to
set my teeth upon the edge

open to a new species of
color capable of containing

or erasing one's own
blurred boundaries

BRUME

smoke crouches
          before standing

          let us look for what
wants notice

snow falling
                    soundless as

                    a single sheet

                    your pause before crying

          out   again
fill up   for

here i widen
the ladder of vision
a book by Brandeis
          who loved Dante
                    (and maybe Montale)
          who wanted to wring the neck of eloquence
                    (never muted under some sacred scanty veil)

her breath smoke-shaped and absurdly human

GOLDENROD

We string
A hammock
Test the balance
Between desire
And wicked thought
With words cut from
A frozen field of rain
The heart you say is
General *sans* army
This world I say
Is winter snake
A spirit apple

How many

Oceans = 1 poem

Hard ground + 2 flowers
Multiply fields of canary tourmaline

Gather symmetrical circles
Bound by bales of burning hay

ARGENT

I rode each small apocalypse
Slyly as a fish in slack water
Beating twilight into scales
Of slivery verse turned
Ingenious by air
Into a chorus of carillon
Bells of winter moon

EXPLAINING PAY PHONES

It can't be a snow globe or those painted horses
From some Nordic land or the circle of angels
Spun by candle flame. Stained glass Shrinky
Dink ornaments or the blobby clay bells way
Too heavy for the annual evergreen to support.
Much ephemerality lingers in this sensation
Staying up all night listening for the miracle
A happy childhood arriving in red
Fur and generous intention. I was
Supposed to write about something
Anachronistic. The locked gate
At the top of the stairs...
Memory rattling the metal

WOOD-FACE

Mr. Stevens found his necessary
Angel in a bowl of venetian glass

But why not the wing-like linen
Serviette outstretched as a glove?

The unstill composition behind
Which we hide the jolt of form

On my side table sits a brutalist
Napoleon in brushed steel

A slingshot abaft his ship of state
Eying the red cows of diablo valley

Their square faces shaded by purple
Pierce right through him

HOW TO WRITE A POEM

Spill words into two non-metallic columns
Sift sugar into one; salt the other.
Wring hands. Set aside.

Pour gin into tumbler
A dash of bitters
Grind imagination
Shake with confidence
Pinch fear.
Increase tempo
Change tempo
Remove punctuation

kneeeeeeeed to taste
Mutter about modernism
            add space   (breath)

        pretension / precaution / presentation
                verbal / vocal / visual
  being / knowing / willing

what are the words one can never say

Assemble all objects before the mirror
Speak *luminous*, wink and apologize
To the fleeting I on the other side

MOST SEARCHED

After Rilke

Aren't we supposed to live our way
Into the answers, lost in the lonesome
Embrace of questions we are not
Fully open to understand

What does the price of petrol
Have to do with ways to help Ukraine
Why does Miami's curiosity about flying
Squirrels make me think of insurrectionists

This has been such a hard few years and two
Days ago was the winter solstice, half-sibling
To another swallowed child of Zeus, one raging
Bomb cyclone before the year turns new again

I love a man with an archaic smile
Alabaster, spice, candles
Today is today is today

IN AN UNNAMED CITY

Who pressed play? The branches are sending up strange sounds, courting my daydreams with fountains, small change twinkling beneath the green film. I soar through the sky like socks in search of a third wheel. The very weather is disarrayed. Alack. Alas. Aloha. I have assigned myself the task of breaking every rule. Never name the rubber ducky. The squeak from the gyre. Ghost of a bluff. I consider only one moment of rest before the statue of midwinter explodes. Stars as from an envelope torn fall across my knees. Beauty's bruise like a brilliant brushstroke.

SABLE

For Zachary Holt Smith

A figure darts beneath the black
Glassy surface of a frozen lake
Darker than the ice that plies
Its tricks with light and sound

In older days, people told tales of such spirits
Otter Kings who would, when captured, grant
Any wish to be set free - or could bestow
If prized, the power of invincibility

Choices are seldom so simple.
Under every chin lies a small point
Of vulnerability - thin like the frosty
Rime we may fall through

To skate sleek and lithe across
An underdream of mirrored time
Searching four-chambered caves
For walls that wish to be windows

Here is what I've discovered about the pear
It is the only fruit that ripens from the inside out
The secret is to rest your finger very gently near
The neck. This is how. We choose each other.

FALL POEM

not long awake
she leaves the warmth
of home to lope the lanes
in the ancient frost-hung way

she parts darkness
switches on the gaze that seeks
no object beyond otherwise
the crackled lichen clinging

unripe to bark, to branch
to bough tenderly traversed
she treads tapestries of bosky
debris which lie upon the floor

floating like glass slippers
each a frozen needle of pine
gathers music from the puddles
Winds ribbons with flowering time

trails of cobwebs and dust
sing out again
the riot of Autumn
has arrived, is home

OCHEROUS

Among the bodice rippers
sheet music
manuals on modern love
a pilgrim book of prayer, lies
one lost summer's field guide
full to the brim with pressed
botanical specimens palely smoldering
atop the bonfire   flames lick-lick
lick-lick
they go savoring the boneless
dry-blotted memory of meadow & maypole
petals fused to fan the news of another century
briefly they bloom again in the oxidized air

to take one final turn towards our original sun
their seeds as hard as stone

INDIGO TWILIGHT

Man steps from the grassy field
You know little of his journey
Or the litanies he is followed by
Soundtracks to interior tours and
Matchless keys to all he's tined

Notes you never learned to play
Reverberate upon the glass slider
Left open for his entry and wait
Long lifetimes in the juddering
Quaver of abalone wine

Rare sips of him like a drowning
Tie his shoes in irreversible lines
So the double syntax of your palms
Can cross a distance farther than miles
Purely lain at uneven intervals

The intonation of a promise
You mimic in the hollow
Of a cloudless cave
Taper of a single track
Sky, trace animals

Bring me your complex fire
I will move the one stone
To help it burn better

THE METAMORPHOSIS OF ANDROMEDA

It's hard to think in terms of four billion
Years or countless galaxy miles, lifetimes
When one highway formed a lifeline

Between you and I.
Rusted storefronts, trucks,
Crackling hills and brassy steer

I imagine my hair spread across your pillow
My body stretched against your back
Our instruments of touch an infinite solace

Some golden web
Long extinct from our species
Tangles with sea stars, sky stars, laughter

As rocks slay the monster
Twisted in its own tail to
Become the one chameleon

SCIENCE MATTERS

All mammals have a clitoris
What of lizards and birds?
Everyone knows that snake
Sex is non-consensual ergo
The mythical hemiclitores
Bears no bona fides. All
Scientists are firm on this
Point, especially as they
Are predominantly the male
Members of their own species
They may not share the forked
Genitals of a male snake but
As for tongues, well, then there
Are the prickly spines to match.
Low and behold what once was
Believed to be vestigial has now
Been confirmed as functional. Olé!
Nerves and erectile tissue discovered
By female scientists (naturally) reveal
All that wrapping and rubbing of tails
Was not a one-way show. It wasn't her
Skin to shed but the hysteria of Victorian
Men who put bloomers on lamb chops
And blushed at the sight of piano legs

GREEN THOUGHT,
BLUE SHADE

I brush the letter's neutral imprimatura

A woman with her arms crossed appears

Ask if all the branches aren't weak with dance

Not skyward leaving

A soft shell has held her

Gets lost to the great listening

Her head tilts from portrait

To landscape

Appellation:

Self in a self-made glade

A GOD SWALLOWS A FLY

The screech brought traffic to a stop
A parliament of horns filled the air

The man to our left exited his vehicle
He sat on a felled and rotting log and wept

A woman walked by with no shoes
Arms of wet sheets and soaked to the bone

A child shook a small pillow and from its torn edge
Feathers rained down like pink confetti

Wing beat wildflower ocean wall
Eyes open to the wind

PROPHECY

Nobody
Nobody
Nobody

Here is a basket of sap
Here is the fall in the path
Where soil dreams of being a forest
Dry wind braids the branches naked
A school of leaves take off

Body
Body
Body

Fruit of the mountain peony cracks
Light across the shallow seabed
You sail towards the opening

RED VERÓNICA

In memory of Jack Hirschman

Halt your wicked mockery
O shiny bronze facsimile
Frozen at the base of Wall Street

No breathing bull would meanly
Dip to a cowardly cape of green
Innocent to the rhythm of greed

It would charge the razor's edge
Pull strength from nostril to animal heart
Hot with fury from the barbs

Of fortunes compounded.
Bombs still scattering.
But it's not from you they run

Stamp stamp upon ground
Loudly pounding as brave bell rung
Rolling the *rrrrs* of revolution
In a thousand languages

To the false deity, you sing out:

People, there is nothing to fear
The poets we are here!
We bring love bright as a red scarf
corrida redoble corrida redoble

Dearest Jack:
Even lying on your back
You are marching

CERTAIN MOTIONS, SEPIA

There is no casual solitude
to slips its hand in yours
as a wave rakes the sand

What can the small icy heart of the comet feel as it nears the sun or the celestial body as it stows its sail into the oriflamme of ocean

Does the tadpole detect loss or gain as his tail lessens to yield limbs

Isn't every trail of a sequence a subsequence of that sequence

a magnetic field may shimmer in sheets of color
your skin shivers like the petal

We see that you have come to seek a new way
What shall you do?

Mathematically perfect, equal as the sum that divides you,
more mysterious than infinity or the scent of fruit under glass
fog condensed, white as a ghost rose
Do not wait for thunder
the storm must break within
your eye too acts as lightning rod

Watch for the intake of the air as it enters the lung of the mountain. Taste of the green leaf made russet on the tongue.

Do you hear laughter quavering in the dark?

There must be no fixed points. Do not trust a map (nor carry a compass).

The passage opens with the only line that cannot be written.

In your hand is the five-cornered fruit.
Its ink moves as a river. You hear only hue.
Trailing dust and vapor
An unfamiliar constellation appears
            It is not the sphere

                        but
                                    the

                                                bounce

IRRIDESCENCE

For Chris Buck

Caught yesterday
In the act of calling
An uncured face to meet
The cardinal winds of the sea
You watched infinite waves
Hook their savage rhythms
To the bluest cry of the sun

Needles of salt
Spin & scuttle
Glass marbles
Filled with sky

They recede
As you plant
Wet-kneed
One by one

A seed

AEGEAN POOLS

A body does not forget its first
feelings, the glare of sun-bleached stone
Thumbs bent in anemone array

Breathe here

Circadian increments
Cross-hatched adjectives
Peel plant to their center

Did I invent this little corner of myth?

I read again what is written above

Caption it *sign language*

With the numb ache of idle hands

SPRING POEM

with wings of equal size and shape   tapered close
to the body   a sort of elegant   *damsel*
would you call me   forth   or *fly*
for a farther window
where those of staggered span dwell
climb up!   o'*here be dragons*
these braids   (meaning also sudden movement)
bronze spears   dry-lit
become
fate's iridescence   on the wind   yet not
momentary
true confessions:

when first i beheld you
skim the water like a sea plane
dip your shoulder to the pool   (how i longed to glide
towards that secret
(spring) of a touch
i cannot name
(just listen for the whir)

focus: shift the we   from object to essence
cradled from pretext to pollination
stretched to send forth
stronger stems
flights of turnstone
gills opening
&   immediately exotic,   possibly the last known
here and hungry   leap   this is

TRUE STORY

Walking sideways
One to the other leg
Says never would
I block your path
Parent-like, I think
They seem as twins
Inching across the sand
To the plastic pail
Full of salt water
Lined with teeth

NO WORDS ON THE WIRELESS

Irish folk dancers
Held arms close
To their bodies
Upright
Even in wartime
Not so much to follow
As to make this bare
Little protest an act
Of loud mercy

AN EXPERIMENT WITH TIME

Nothing stands still, except in our memory.
— Philippa Pearce

Far past the asparagus beds and bean poles
Raspberry cane, gooseberry & black current
A small slip of paper rests in a row of rhubarb

Between the closing moments of midnight and before
One minute past lies the lost hour in which your whole
Life takes shape, out of regular order

The bell strikes thirteen
As a splinter in the heart
A pip pushed to the surface

BODY SWEATS

Snake a divide at 120th
Through the hum of city car queues
Excitedly aghast as the baroness
Elsa von Feytag-Lorinhoven hauls a urinal
To the funeral of culture
Snapping turtles tick like lilies
Every fountain pen has exploded
The octopi collapse into love-clutch
Smoking from every tentacle
No one applauded
Not even her mind

INTERFERENCE BLUE

flesh with flecks of cobalt
first underpainting now a crowd

violet seeds the verges
obscured, too close
a bumble blend of Azureum Allium
like a line of oars in the ocean

neither whale nor truth
moves in a straight line
there is no one
wasted thing
to pull up
crawl out of

another you
a brush combed through
silvery saplings with poor tinting strength
hints of viridescence and spintronics
storage of hidden energy
weed from easy view
an additional dash of
trace magnetism

everything to remain
for the tiny terrorists of springtime
bloom
urge us to the floor
I did the shattering
eagle clutches dove clutches flight

(owe nobody your bright shards)

SUMMER POEM

We met in wet grass in the early morning and lay there until the sky shone with stories. A Cat's Eye Nebula, the Tadpole Galaxy, Celestial Eagle and Swan. Summer's asterism only 17 million miles away.

Side by side, our fingers stitched into baskets, we cradle our own thoughts, touching only at bent elbows. Our feet bare. I want to tell you, though I'm not sure that I can really explain, about the time I met a mystery alone in the woods. Which one, you ask? There are different ways to answer that, as with any question. None say enough.

I begin to count what I can of these terrestrial stars. Each lightning bug produces a chemical reaction inside its abdomen. Bioluminescence occurs when oxygen and the enzyme luciferase meet. It's a cold light generating little actual heat. Like a ghost lamp. Such facts are another way of trying to add up the disparate moments that make a life.

The latin word *lucifer* means morning star or light-bringing, if used as a descriptor. I suppose people do change. Even angels. Even this garden. Yet I know that if I let my smallest toe lean into yours, right now, I will feel warm all over. Somehow this is everything and enough.

TANGERINE

We overheard them
Raising the oval half-light
High above our glowing zeppelin

A taste as fine powder
Neither bitter nor sweet bore fruit
From the hallway of scrambled grief

Some few hap-hazard angels liaised
Their intricate fright-filled anecdotes
Above a cobweb parapet

Wings gestured in the fashion
Of the season's espalier
Like something less impossible
To shoulder than these voice

Solstice is announced
Ferns walk from lip to lip

CHARTREUSE

Woodland assemblage of flora and fauna
Wardrobed in retro-reflective safety values
Sashay the monastic routeways of woodfrog
Quillwort and waterclover. A looking glass

Of False Venus offers refuge
From seasonal flowing, from fish predation.
The *ifs* of colony or monastery are immaterial
We all begin ephemeral

It is only within the circle of snakebites that we flow
Past sirens singing our fluorescent destiny
Lover, your music has unbound me
Inundation (filling winter)

Desiccation (spring flowering)
Evapotranspiration (summer dry)
I am here to fall
Languaged for the taking

When I say slowly, melt
I am interested in mostly
Your impermeable layer
The ungraded soil of spirit

Native only to you

13 PALMERSTON ROAD

Slim rectangle of galley kitchen
I'd venture down in wool socks
With the taste of brown sugar
Already melting on my tongue
She's set down my plastic purple
Bowl and ladle in the porridge
Turning her back to allow me
Free reign in the administration
Of the raw and treacly topping

I expect she handled me differently
In the days of the old Parsonage
When her English husband kept
A level of box hedge formality
Before her haughty Chinese
Upbringing went the way of rose
Petals in the garden.

She'd still mutter at the Labor politicians
and hooped earrings on the Americans
At Wimbledon as though he
Were still next to her on the settee
Not the messy wild child of the daughter
She hadn't raised. And I loved her
Summers on the small plot of lawn.

SITKA SPRUCE

For Sujin Nam

It began with pentimenti
Dusty tracks in the empty room
Of an eastern town where once
I was quite sad

But this was not to be my confession
— The poem inside the poem —
For that I must back myself in
As a way to face forward

Winding my way towards what is true
You have sent me a photo of your studio
I spy the glow of a skull of brass, a circular spray of yellow orchids arrayed on your upright

Reminds me of a vintage eraser
Its bright fanning brush used to wipe away mistakes made on a manual typewriter -
Organs and harpsichords are instruments with multiple manuals

Perhaps pedalboards and keyboards are like people
They respond differently to touch. This leads me to wonder
How it would feel to lie beneath Schubert's piano
Trio in e-flat major

To absorb *Andante con moto*
From the ground up as a caress
Considering that I want my love to feel
Me similarly as both lively and tender
As a red-shouldered hawk
As a fawn by the fence

These are real things that have touched us
and this is the heart of the poem:

Never to be careless
Ever to be ready
Each moment. This moment
Is a body breathing

Listening for you
To say yes

FORTUNE COOKIE

For Pedro Jiménez

My dinner with a fictionalized version of myself
Begins without sacramental element
Ends without being

- Buried alive on Halloween night
- Soundtracked for three pianos
- Paralyzed by boredom, or
- Greeted with universal acclaim

Between courses
The soul gives in to gossip
Going through the motions,
Plates are cleared
A napkin is thrown to
Flaunt confidence, dare gravity
I hear the satisfying flutter of sonic defiance

Surely this is a celebration, but how will I cover the check?

Sidereal to another act of freedom
My spirit forest stands poised in second position   ready to perform the rites of spontaneity
Cliche is off- menu

Confess:
You are a mute star fruit
Feel shame for this easy rhyme
Pale sylph of the fall garden
Distilled to a gilded finish

Avow:
The dream of all nows is heady aroma
Words a drizzled sublapse of atoms
Stippling the shore like leopard waves devouring their own dithyrambs

A digestif of life itself
Savored vicarious oddity
I will have nothing less
A bent stinger, a tossed hat, the last laugh

FULL SPECTRUM

Yellow is nearest to the light
According to Goethe for whom blue
Carries a principle of darkness

What then would we from this jigsawed
Scene of solstice and supra-seasonal
  artifice
Decoct of the pilgrim-protagonist

She has again upon another bed
of raw cotton flung her comedy of moody hues.
The emulsion wanders the white space on feet of
precious chroma

Down to the western edge until at last
Alive at peace and whole beyond
        Washout & wipe away

A round clear pool of purpose
        strokes to the all-mine horizon

What foreground could resist her proximity?

Own that you do not belong outside of this scene
Even the shadow of the wind dances backwards

UNDER / PRESSURE

For Ana Teresa Fernández

We brace against what is fluid
Molten core or brittle border
I get technical when nervous
Surging, sinking, subsiding
Lodestoned to the brink of climax
I touch your hottest center
Imagining the exceptional
From an emptiness less elastic than regret
The compound power of two elements
A suspense of azure hands
Air makes anything detachable
But not forever
Raw rare earth rusted by iron and phosphorus
You loosen anchors of possessiveness
Thereby the thinnest heel of grief
Ankles away from annihilation
Can we believe in a more permeable layer of loving
Startled into one we would hold the waves aloft
Pressed Cerulean, Aquamarine, Indigo
Pooled by chartreuse
An unsingled sigh
Feeling its way to fact:

Nothing spills
The imperfect sphere of the earth
Keeps spinning

FLY FISHING

On this last day
That is also the eve of the next
A torrent of concentrated moisture
Called an atmospheric river runs
Heavy on our parched hills.
It is no rare phenomena according
To climatologists but it turns me up-
Side down like the human race
Has shimmied back to the sea
And maybe we should slip
Back on our boney fins
To count up the year's losses
Ending with the news
Of a friend from college
Who drops his wings so he could fly
I remember you on couches and in kitchens
On middle path and between classes
I remember you back in your bluegrass home
Shooting beer cans and playing tennis
I remember you in the ballroom
After the mint julep fountains ran dry
Pull up a chair next to your godmother
To put her feet on your lap and rub them
I remember you choosing an empty golf course
Over a muddy crowded infield &
I remember the laughter of youth
When the end of a term meant nothing
But a list of the good and the bad events
What can I carry from the dustbin of this year?
You are taking up both columns.
I haven't seen you in many years
Now I can conjure your smile from thin air
Like a river flowing towards the greatest ocean
Becoming rain, becoming snow, becoming spring

NOT TO SQUANDER THE GAZING

Sibelius sewed 16 swans into his fifth symphony
coiled brass, flared bell, jets of wingbeat   ecstasy
a loosening madness, a wending desire for footfall
to be loudly lost among nature's syllabic rhythms
I walk outwards where differently barked
and downy enticements
sway even the souls of sprigs
at jest attend to nothing more
than the motif of bouncing oatnuts
>< drum roll >< crescendo ><
announce the coming of a canyon
cut from urban enclave or survives; its ragged opening
a shelter to unaccompanied coyote
goading locals to thorned debate. Wildness at work!
the original occupation of unmetered overtime
only always greenness and change
the pre-enlightenment of fern, of snail,
wordless mossy spur, you sun-harvester,
needle me with pine's silent seductions
teach the interior foliage
no coda but weed extravagance

QUINTESSENCE

For Cheryl Haines

Æther may be a place of oscillating rainbows
A region where strange angels go to evade
Mortal chaos and the endless self-inflicted
Catastrophe of human longing. Perhaps.

Seductress of the sun, daughter of time
Offspring of the stars. How much I still revere
Your name, the pure word. Grace, forgiveness.
Some hidden thread that keeps us whole and kind

Two massive objects - our will and the world - attract
Each other gravitationally. It's spooky how closely we tug
Without needing to touch. Anticipation of rhapsody is more
Than many ever know of regions not visible to the naked eye

You are most real because truth is obscured by artful clouds
I know you as beauty. You answer to art even when unwatched

To be breath itself is to remember light flickering on the
darkened cave of the sky and imagine the absolute violet of hope
consenting to be ours.

PORCELAIN

1.
A treasure chest of rabbit's feet
A smell like burnt hair and clove
And from below as he loomed
Above me with a drill, the man
Who tortured my teeth, stole
My smile and sense of safety
Would ask after my family
Tell me to brush frequently
As my gums bled

2.
Freshman summer I discovered
I could eat so little I was almost
Happy like an air-light bird or a wire
Or a real woman stepping through
A block of stone into the body she
Had hoped against hope to occupy
Then down on her knees to pray
It could stay that way, even if
More teeth would fall

3.
The first half of life is trying
To drop the stitches of suffering
To brush away the plaque before
It takes over like mistletoe
On a hosting apple tree
The rest is remembering as hard
As you can because the zombie you
Needs to feel what it is not to be
A cavity in the cosmos

TWO IN A BALANCE OF LONG EXPOSURE

Through a whisper of silence and foam
From the shadow shell of your body

You emerge robed not in destiny but innuendo
Whether polished steel or palpitating flesh

The arching self always reveals its secret nave
As every natural form carries its own cathedral

Fluted ribs, the blades of your splendor
Shelter an extravagance akin to innocence found

Sea is to sky as skin is to soul as seeking is to song
Rejoice! storm clouds will taper to brightening arrows

Pressed as such against the naked light of the world
Your eyes grow liberated of expectation

Focus reselects for the celebration of chasms
Foreground, aperture, tireless monument

Wide western depths fall upon you like a star
As my lips upon yours melt all distance

Embrace the bullseye echo of dynamic heat
The stranger who knows you by heart

THE FLOATING CHEST

After Robert Frost

Along shabby streets where painted faces
Once danced furious carnal patterns
Twin lights judder into darkness

The mediating sea rages to my right
To the left, branches whip my cheek
To the purr of some ancient exotic insect
Whose shade-shifting color I can almost recall

A cry across the riverstone macadam
The rooftops of grass glistening with fish
I place my ear to the tumbling wave
I open my mouth to its music

GIOCONDA

The secret of a smile is in the eyes
Keep your windows clean & closed

Sweet solitude shuts centuries of stares
Flashbulbs dissolve into black wolves

No one really looks anymore
To survey the soul's surrender

Influencers ignore innovation for cliché
Blurred background becomes setting

Any resemblance to the Madonna
As out of vogue as peripheral vision

Apollinaire and Picasso were accused
Of stealing me, but they read my look

True, a woman wishes to be more than
Her frame and paint, I flew for seconds

Strange sister, this time
Swallowed by afterimage

The imaginary landscape
The innocent star's gaze

UNTITLED (FEARFUL BOOKCASE)

For Sahar Khoury

Revolution
Is that all you want?
Like lines of Loy's manifesto
Inadequate the wrench, the censor
Thieved from the empty nest of truth
A vital ghost lined in feathers
Titles wired to broken wing
Exiled like a flower garland chasing spring
Warships that prostitute themselves before
Wood-fired mystery, always, always
At a loss to worship free
Here now, drop a knee
My heart is a furnace
To burn down fear
Kinship kindling
The cracked moor
The creaky door
Weighty tether
Anchor of me
To you

PURGATORY OF LOST CONNECTIONS

For Charlie Pendergast and Kevin Connor

Enthusiasms of the overhead
announcer sound nothing like
a negligée slipped from hip
to unravel and pool like
some Mayan temple
or the colored bands
of a Frank Stella

if I imagine every roller
bag is a barge upon
the air and every
fixed arm divider
a wing tucked
hermitage
a dovecote
for daffodil

It's been a day
93 degrees
in purgatory
in Phoenix
(would i fly
from ashes!)
for fog forgivingly
to be resurrected
from this Marriot

O here are my coins
attend me ferryman
towards the clouds
above the whispers
of this hollow horse

my road has been a long one
will I be old before I reach
my island? Shall I somehow
learn to be less a fool?

no one seeks
a kingdom
of laundry bags
and lint rollers tho
shapes may shift
into dragons sprawled
upon their treasures
cloister books beneath
their tails and belly
i grasp my own
knees & beg
shelter

i will take your mini bus
i will board your steel umbrella
let white lavender speak
the mysteries of the mesa
concrete, chile pepper, las luces
de los alamos blink towards us
the question is an empty envelope
slipped beneath my door
as i sleep i dream as i live
the sounds of the seaside
open my eyes to thee
Hestia of the southwest
what pleasure
what joy

IN THE SUNRISE ARC

We are floating in a realm of time 900 million years before the big bang as our universe keeps expanding. More than twice as hot as the sun and a million times more luminous, we are lucky to be living behind a wrinkle in spacetime so massive it wraps the fabric of the galaxy. Stars as massive as Earendel often have companions. We know from its colors that a cooler, redder light has been stretched by the expansion of the universe to wavelengths longer than all but one, the strongest telescope can detect. This is its mate. A bonded pair. I am taking liberties with science, as ever, bending and stretching it to metaphor, but I wanted to give you something that wouldn't fit in a box. A gift that could never be contained or stored away. I wanted to tell you that you make my world so much larger than I could have imagined. I don't need gravitational lensing or to look through Hubble's eye to see how the light in your eyes makes my day stellar. I love being wrapped in the fabric of your universe.

TWO

She draws lines like horizons
Or waves with invisible endings

He pulls the brush from nave to foreground
A heavy load of sunlight comes closer

Her touch gave the lift of fish
Their descending slash of gill and sail

Sea curves and his hand is full of sand
Bell wall of the body moving towards sound

Seven letters suppose suggest a lost alphabet
A series of ribbed symbols punched through sky

Star tunnels collapsed to prevent an exit
Fugitives from white-knuckle thirst

She sharpens a moon against her hip
He crosses bird with drum and weeping

SUNROOM WHISPERS

I miss our mornings. Light coming on as neighbors walk their dogs and watch you mix paint directly on canvas. You're impetuous and seem to the outside world unafraid in these moments. But I hear your muttering self-reproach. You try too many things, you say, and never get good at any one of them. Then the thing resolves into itself. Addition and subtraction. Downright and circuitous. Color over color over color. You are not done dismantling. You are not done doing what wakes you all the way up. Even failure can be an extravagance, an enabler. To be bewildered is sometimes to turn a corner on the journey Cry out with those who went this way before: *The sea! The sea!*

Tamsin Spencer Smith, 2022

Tamsin Spencer Smith was born in Cambridge, UK and has lived in the San Francisco since 1997. She earned a BA with highest honors in English from Kenyon College and an. MA in international affairs from The Fletcher School at Tufts University.

This is her fifth collection of poems. She has also published a novel and frequently writes art reviews and catalogue essays. Her paintings have been exhibited throughout the Bay Area, including solo shows at Adobe Books Backroom Gallery, Danielle SF, Upper Market Gallery, and PurpleMaroon. She is keyboardist and co-songwriter for the indie band WUNDERCAT.

Smith is managed in all endeavors by Moriarty (Mo), her marmalade tabby cat.

THE PAGE POETS SERIES

Number 1
Between First & Second Sleep by Tamsin Spencer Smith

Number 2
The Michaux Notebook by Micah Ballard

Number 3
Sketch of the Artist by Patrick James Dunagan

Number 4
Different Darknesses by Jason Morris

Number 5
Suspension of Mirrors by Mary Julia Klimenko

Number 6
The Rise & Fall of Johnny Volume by Garrett Caples

Number 7
Used with Permission by Charlie Pendergast

Number 8
Deconfliction by Katharine Harer

Number 9
Unlikely Saviors by Stan Stone

Number 10
Beauty Will Be Convulsive by Matt Gonzalez

Number 11
Displacement Geology by Tamsin Spencer Smith

Number 12
The Public Sound by Marina Lazzara

Number 13
Record of Records by Rod Roland

Number 14
Strangers We Have Known by John Briscoe

Number 15
Cutting Teeth by Jesse Holwitz

Number 16
Other Scavengers by Lauren Caldwell

Number 17
Cueonia by Jesse Holwitz

Number 18
In the Museum of Hunting and Nature by Cynthia Randolph

Number 19
A New Species of Color by Tamsin Spencer Smith

Made in the USA
Columbia, SC
30 May 2024

36316031R00043